So Rarely
in Our Skins

So Rarely in Our Skins

Robert Moore

The Muses' Company Series Editor: Catherine Hunter
Cover design by Robert Moore and Doowah Design Inc.
Cover painting is "Dédale et Icare" by Charles-Paul Landon
Reproduced with the kind permission of Musée des Beaux-Arts et de la Dentelle d'Alençon (France)
Author photo by Deborah Moore
Printed and bound in Canada

We acknowledge the financial support of the Manitoba Arts Council and The Canada Council for the Arts for our publishing program.

Canadian Cataloguing in Publication Data

Moore, Robert John, 1950-
So rarely in our skins

ISBN 1-896239-89-7

I. Title.

PS8576.O61525S6 2002 C811'.6 C2002-900284-2
PR9199.4.M658S6 2002

J. Gordon Shillingford Publishing
P.O. Box 86, 905 Corydon Avenue, Winnipeg, MB Canada R3M 3S3

for my family

Acknowledgements

Many of these poems have appeared (occasionally in slightly different versions) or are forthcoming in the following journals: *Canadian Author, Descant, The Fiddlehead, Contemporary Verse 2, Gaspereau Review, Ink Magazine, The New Quarterly, Prairie Fire, Pottersfield Portfolio, Wascana Review, Quadrant* (Australia), *The Abiko Literary Quarterly* (Japan). A number of them have also been broadcast on CBC Radio's "Live Poets" series.

A shorter version of "High School Reunion Buffet" won Honourable Mention in *Pottersfield Portfolio's* 1997 Short Poem Contest. An earlier version of this collection received Special Honourable Mention in the 2001 Writers' Federation of New Brunswick Alfred G. Bailey Prize Poetry Manuscript Competition.

I am grateful to the Canada Council for their generous support during the completion of this project. Thanks also to Anne Compton who spoke to many of these poems soon after they'd been sent into the breathing world scarce half made up, and to my editor, Catherine Hunter, for her guidance and enthusiasm.

Table of Contents

Dispossessions

Dead-ends and Celebration

So Rarely in Our Skins

Unfavourable Stars

Inversions of Other Travels

Dispossessions

There is so much Everything
that Nothing is hidden quite nicely.
—W. Szymborska

At the Suggestion of a Dead Poet

a poem is a falling forward into
darkness said robert frost who late
one evening maybe got up from his chair
made his way to the cellar
down to the wet root smell
air the house is slow to breathe
careful from habit on those wicked steps
and there, white haired and bent perhaps
beneath a naked light
considering the weight of a hand
at the end of a length of butcher string
and the way a body
comes loose in the dark
gradually working free of the heart
driven deep as a nail
into the warm pine floor
of the room above

Moon

The second-order moon certainly
interests us. Its odd little take on
illumination our long-standing metaphor
for mutability; goddesses with phosphorous
hearts, arrows they like to name; lighting of choice
for the white-ankled dead whose real motives remain mostly
unclear. A particular moon makes an example
of a cold sky.

The sun *is* of course, but the moon pretty much
has to make it up as it goes along. The pressure of re-
membering suspends the weight of blood over emptiness,
skins black rivers in the brain. The moon is
a quiet mass of contradictions.

Like tonight, with a ceiling high and clear,
present with stars, the moon holds itself apart, dances
behind veils of clouds slight as any occasion. It moons like
nothing; verbs the dark in every cup of bone we tilt
looking up, improvising out there
like nobody's business.

Inspiration: a Triptych

Without horses, we saddle the dogs.
—Syrian proverb

I

I suppose there are streetlights on the road to Damascus.
And at evening, Toyota pick-ups feel their way along. Headlights
whispering long passages of asphalt, on the lookout
for the blue flash of eyes. Stray asses, maybe.
Small calibre holes in the night.

On blindingly hot days streetlights revert to empty scaffolds,
condemned to line avenues through the Holy Land like the same verse
repeated in a thousand parched religions. The punishing work
of making ends meet in a desert.

II

It's unlikely any 'x' marks the spot. No cenotaph
with a brass plate before which to pause.
Here, it might claim,
God Whacked A Jew with Light. Not even
one of those small white crosses we plant beside highways
to remind travellers how easily the fabric between worlds can
part. And really,
you wouldn't want to pin it down.
It's not a place so much as an episode; a metaphor for
absolute travel or exhausted plans; mind driven through
its limits, shot out some other side:

Thrown suddenly back, Saul strikes his
skull against adamantine ground. A dozen or so
cartoon stars arrive to orbit his cruciform eyes,
stitched to the air like butterflies,
scraps of yellow cloth.

III

What are we shown? I stand on the porch
under loose cairns of stars, the dog
chasing its nose over soft spears of lawn.
Each of us is touching base, breath offering
temporary solutions to that older matter
of cold black air.

And isn't this the same moon Saul left for Paul
on the nightstand
that time he went out for a drive
and never came home?

Abracadastra

I

Adumbrating a familiar logic, history has not neglected to record that the
first son of Johannes Kepler was born with "seriously disfigured genitals."
Kepler, apparently no looker himself, had only recently accomplished a
reshaping of the heavens when this prodigious birth occurred.
The precise nature of the son's deformity is unknown.
It's a mystery, albeit on a homely scale.

II

Kepler demolished a belief that had held firm since the time of Pythagoras
by demonstrating that the planets—those various acolytes of stars—
notwithstanding the ostensible redundancy of their devotions
behaved erratically; as in: *Planets move in elliptical orbits*
with the sun at one focal point.

"When he learned that Galileo had seen four moons orbiting Jupiter
he decided that Mars would have two. Why two? Because
it would be mathematically harmonious.... He happened
to be right about Mars, but that was simply
a coincidence."

III

In a way that cannor help but fascinate, the tale of the curious
birth defect of Kepler's son, apocryphal or not, rehearses by way
of condensation the myth of Prometheus and of Adam's fall.
The punishment for stealing fire (sacred knowledge)
from the heavens, and the shame associated with such an act
(at least in the instance of the Judeo-Christian Adam), are re-
configured—in a minor miracle of displacement—in the flesh
of Kepler's 'innocent' boy.

How foolish we have been all these ages to believe Our Father
so inept a Maker as to nail the Earth like a penny
to His own Forehead!

Two liverish elliptical little pricks
flanking one enormous ball?

In the Garden

Every summer since we bought this house
I have killed at least one snake in the yard
never more than two

There is an implement for this
doubling as a walking stick
cut from a length of striped maple
called *snake maple* by some locals
for the pattern of its green and fleshy bark
thick as a child's wrist

I kill them on behalf of my wife
who loves to garden
but hates a certain order of surprise

I go at them with an atavistic fury
the sort I usually reserve for a rival god;
something just comes over me

I stop swinging only when their jaws
come completely unhinged

The bodies I throw onto the flat roof of the shed
imagining as I turn away
the ease with which birds will work them
into ceremony

If I bury them the dog will dig them up
no matter how secretly, deep, or many times
I fit them in the ground

Something in this dog compels it to walk around
with a rotting snake for a tongue

It remains a mystery to me
    a) how he finds them, and
    b) what he's out to achieve

I'd ask him   I would
But can you imagine the look I'd receive

Rocky

alone and clumsy dancing
at the loose end
of a knotted vein of pedigree
our short-legged, thick-coated
castrated dog

all summer long and into the fall
he makes a perfect spectacle
throws chattering voles
high into the air
out of the tall grass
and madly frolics after

this various blood
this singular hunt
all dead-ends
and celebration

The Deer

Standing in the backyard snow
four white-tailed deer in broad daylight
arranged in various attitudes
I almost said like lawn ornaments
but for the way they resisted
with their liquid eyes.

They regard the house with me in it
as one might something
timed to go off.

The deer, having come this far,
will only come so close.

There is so much magic in their just being here
that I put on my coat and go out to them
with a silver arrow, and each
offers me its gentle heart
because it has to, and we're all
a little ambivalent about this
but we bend to it
because we have to
        and the next snow
completely heals the wide red path
back to the house.

But I have no silver arrow
so I don't go out,
and the deer can only wait so long.

I keep the dogs in
that whole afternoon.
They are housebroken, you see,
lost the sense of how things
are done. They'd chase the first deer they saw
from here to Kingdom come.

Charlie Parker

crows in white sky
jazz of their phrasing
murder of verbs on winter air

Grapevine, Scriptorium, February

tangle of veins
against the house
what's left
of last year's
tumid hand

the odd grapes
hanging in
black as sin
since nothing
came for them

taste the ends
of a monk's fingers

Let Daddy Tell the Story

yesterday
claims my little angel
she went into the woods
and slapped a monster
really hard
on the face

she weighs in
at about thirty-five pounds
fists about the size
of plums—two of them together
might make one heart

of course
this is less than the truth

there are no such things as monsters
and she's never been to those woods

from the window where I'm standing
I clearly see the field of snow
lying out there
unbroken

there isn't a mark on it
none at least that shows

Hallowe'en

as soon as it got dark
they turned up

and not just a few

    superheroes, pirates, demons
    ghosts with pink fingers
        out for sweeties to chew

            this year's crop even included
            Kanga and Roo

well we could hardly wait to spring on them
this awful old trick we still do

(after all you'll recall
it's our evening too)

oh but how good each was
in the end

really
        right the way through

down to that milk-sour last breath
in each little shoe

March

month
snow actually rots. coats
act like they somehow got wind
of the divorce. appetite for colour so
pronounced that men at war with the speechless
woods dream of sliding their tongues under
axes. telephones ring every nail in the lid
of the house deeper in and guess what
it's only luscious April calling
to remind you it's still
the cruelest
month.

The Day Ghost

Help me, the ghost said, catching my wrist as
thin fingers of shadow circle the well of a dish.

Been in the house for ages, sucking curtains for light,
wary of the phone, weeping into the night.

But you just got here, I claim, notwithstanding our inventory
of failed gestures, inaccurate smiles in the crust on the mirror.

Yes, I appreciate that, said the ghost, eyes on mine like
edge on a knife. *But I really need to get on with my life.*

You know, this reminds me, I said, *of the difference between*
silver and tinsel. I don't know why it popped into my head.

Pathos, said the ghost. *You wrote it down in your little book.*
'In case I forget,' you said, *'I'll know just where to look.'*

What would I do without you, I said. *Now let's go remake*
the bed. Later, for fun, we can lie in it too.

Postcard to My Wife in Another City

dear

here/rain
stops spring
cold in its tracks

drapes wet
over windows
several layers thick

but I trust

green ink somehow sends through
the iron veils winter left

and you are precisely
there
where you said

in the eggshell city

on the scrabbled edge of the hotel bed
shoulders coming forward
to wrap the heart

contemplating
the prospect of an afternoon
open wide enough to drive a wedding through

yours

Telling Time

I used to gather one set of grandparents, stopped cold
in several photographs, into the small of my hands
like prayers.

The law of non-contradiction worked open their fields,
pitched shadow through churchyards, spread the yellow ribs
of barns soaked with mornings early in the twentieth century.

Then, as now, the proper names for insects organized breath
into small categories; stars on black water got lost
in thought. My daughter,

whose forehead tastes of stone and light, asks me how to tell time.
Sometimes it helps to think of it as a face, I suggest,
with more than one tongue.

Lines out of Winter

Should I send more poems, leave them lying
in snow: red knots, odd flakes of tongue.

Next you'll send word demanding an audience
while I'm not at liberty, stuck as I am.

Translations of our situation continue to appear,
You'd think this would make some difference.

There was no point in our further discussing the Russians
notwithstanding such beautiful, unlikely names.

Spring will describe these fields another way; winter
is running out of openings.

Yes, both dogs have stayed with me, eyes patient
as holes in a wall.

When a man came to the door asking for you
my response took the form of a scythe.

Putting a name to every bone in the human hand
you had me at a wonderful disadvantage.

Yesterday, for no reason, I thought of you, sitting
perfectly alone, taking a sentence apart.

To the best of my recollection, we never made plans
in this house, and so, I remain.

If you decide to come, you might address me
by another name, given this awful country.

Dead-ends and Celebration

Most of the words we have are not the words
for what we really want.

—Charles Baxter

Watches

Oh a new watch has the cleanest hands of all.
See, every spoke of the morning sun is wearing one.

If you just watch a watch, you become a sort of performance artist
offering suggestive insights into the failure of the English language.

Bulova is too beautiful a word to languish
on a list of copyrighted brand names. Bulova. Bulova.

People replace watches either before they stop working
or after. There can be no exception to this rule.

If you buy someone a watch, write this on the card:
Please find enclosed the most precious gift of all.

With every new watch, you are given a little time
to start all over again.

If you die soon after the purchase of a watch,
you're apt to be buried with it as a kind of joke.

There is nothing in the stomach of a new watch.
It is looking forward to your arm and all of its appetites.

Persons who keep their watches on during sexual intercourse
are bound to arouse suspicion.

Wearing someone else's watch always constitutes
an invasion of someone's privacy.

The statistical research indicating that persons who refuse to wear watches
live longer and more productive lives than you or me is hereby deemed
fantastical.

If you ever lose a watch, try not to picture the following:
one of the Fates holding it up to her nose and savouring your scent.

Even a stopped watch is accurate twice a day.
If you think that the person who came up with that one is named Reg or even Alice
you could easily be wrong until the end of time.

There should be a rest home for old watches:
they have been through so much and are owed some sort of an explanation.

Why don't they make a digital watch that ticks anyway
for old time's sake?

A surprising percentage of suicides remove their watches before taking the plunge.
Most of the time, this makes absolutely no sense to me at all.

Bulova.

Bulova.

From The Golden Book of Bovinities

We are nowhere near as calm as we probably appear.
It's just that our minds are elsewhere.

Pound for pound, our eyes are no more expressive
than puddles of dark brown glass.

From the highway they imagine us
nosing toy cars through the grass.

There's just no getting around the fact that certain mornings
in the dew-wet fields are better than others.

When they lean over the fence to shout 'moo' at us
it isn't nonsense we shout back.

Breeds are named for places, which is why the Holstein
keeps coming up with maps of anywhere else.

Only when skin develops a sense of industry
will it truly fit like a glove.

On the way to slaughter we advise keeping your head down
and your thoughts pretty much to yourself.

The heart of even an undersized cow
still makes quite a handful.

As evening approaches, discussion inevitably turns
to the topic of greener pastures.

Among other things, Prince Edward Island is famous for its cows.
The bitterness of its horses alone must be spectacular.

Keep your money in your horns. It's the last place
they think to look.

On more than one occasion men have used us for sexual intercourse.
We must seem the very souls of discretion. At least from behind.

Pigs have a saying: *There are no ironists in the abattoir.*
For pigs, that's not bad.

It is widely believed that even our tongues end up on their plates.
Naturally, our feelings on this subject are very difficult
to put into words.

We do not explain pictures, we explain remarks about pictures

Vincent's Chair with his pipe and *Gauguin's Armchair*
by Vincent Van Gogh; oil on canvas, 1888

ah but you take that moving last season in the so-called "Yellow House" when worldly Gauguin has all but given up on provincial Van Gogh (which the former pointedly now velarizes *hawk* thereby sending the latter alternately flying or packing as juice from the back of his throat) well after the two have taken to throwing colour at one another from behind a series of small canvas walls (critics awarding Gauguin, easily the taller of the two, the early advantage) starting with those protomodernist breakfasts when spattered sleeves tabled various approaches to

morning as a war of nerves or who should play us in a major motion picture called why won't you execute my way or it's not simply a matter of colour that's not what I intoned but the way line can excise the heart from form too oh what nonsense the shape of energy the harmony of brutal extremes shit what fucking merde you're always brushing pass the last of the scrambled I'll show you line pass me a razor can't you anthony quinn of all the lively exchanges these chairs might have had

Famous Artist Descending a Standard Biography

Vincent was an avid reader.

"Books, mostly. Dry, white faces. Indeed, disfigurements
of any kind. Though I found its anachronisms a torment,
The Catcher in the Rye took my heart
apart with its layered dramatizations
of the human situation."

Vincent became obsessed with this image of a serious, sensitive woman.

"It was time to choose another. The combination of her
seriousness and her sensitivity, together
with her willingness to be reduced
to a crude image I would
carry in the pocket
of the trousers
of my mind
for years.

In fact, until that fateful visit to the new Rijksmuseum one October day, late in the nineteenth century."

Vincent's work with Goupil in England had started out well enough but by 1875 he seemed to have lost interest.

"It is 1875 and already I seem to be losing interest in Goupil. I don't know what I expected. And working with another redhead like Nigel is certainly no walk in the park. Though I must say that, even after all these weeks, the flash of his yellow teeth inside that green cloud of cologne in which he always figures gives me such ideas. A day indoors with him and I find I have to go out and attack the fields with my new vocabulary. Though I do find his moustache a convincing touch."

Vincent's letters to Theo in this period became rambling, near-hysterical.

"Hey— I.— Stop! Please. No. What was I saying? Cravat. Sincerely. God help me, what I wouldn't give for a decent burnt umber! No, I take that back!"

One of his coworkers had less favourable memories:

"I've known some sick twists in my time, but this guy was a piece of work. [Pause] Yeah, he sort of kept to himself, mostly. Had this way of looking right through you, even when he was talking to you, which wasn't too often. Eyes like...I don't know...like holes in the world. Know what I mean? This one guy called him 'Vinnie' all the time...you know, bustin' his balls. Well, Vinnie would fix him with those eyes and say—easy as you please, mind you, like it was an honest mistake: 'No, my name is Vincent, as in Vincent van Gogh, the tormented genius.' Hysterical, right? [Pause] Christ, he got beat up *a lot*."

Vincent stayed in the area and continued his work for another whole year, living in the most squalid conditions imaginable.

"'I never imagined it would be this squalid,' he wrote
to his brother. 'It's like someone spent their colourless life
squirrelling sacks of assholes into where the angles meet. Given such
unwholesome conditions, you can imagine how the air is multiplied.

In the closet, under the floorboards,
I suspect a nest.'"

He nursed mangled victims of a mine disaster.

"I cannot even begin to describe to you how complicated these scenes were, but naturally I'll try. First there was my state of mind, given, as you well know, to the rambling and the near-hysterical. Then there were the rooms, ordinary rooms at any other time but now weighed down, their walls sagging, thick with detail. Why, the little so-called closets alone beggar description! Then there was the space unoccupied by that ponce, Nigel. Then there were the men, each of their wounds a crude tear in the canvas behind which worlds erupted and convulsed. Their eyes thickening like the eyes of birds crushed in a fist. To say nothing of the white faces of the children. Thick as pages 57 through 71 of *Catcher in the Rye*, I thought, for some sudden reason, between small unnumbered acts of nursing...."

***There is something inside of me, what can it be?...* (Letter #133 [to Theo], July, 1880)**

"Of course, my notions in this regard keep changing. That is the problem, I think. Change. Mind you, I have something in the pocket of my trousers that does not change. Unless I do first. Which is a comfort. But not always. [Pause] What was I saying?"

He reacted strongly to advice from Tersteeg:

"That's an excellent suggestion, M. Tersteeg! How dare you!"

In Paris, he discovered colour as well as the divisionist ideas which helped to create the distinctive dashed brushstrokes of his later work.

"'Dash it all (as that phoney prick Nigel was so fond of saying), you should come to Paris,' he wrote to M.G. Delsaut. 'They have a thing here called "colour" which will nicely complement any divisionist leanings you were thinking of having. I wonder what effect this visit will have on the brushstrokes of subsequent cogitations? Thoughts?'"

Vincent had a falling out with Mauve:

"The whole thing started with Mauve's grotesque claim, ventured after six too many glasses of cheap pernod, that the more savant one becomes, the greater the degree of naivety possible in the work. When he raised his finger in the air with a flourish and said something about the 'stink of our sapience,'
well, I simply had to act."

He wrote some especially moving and beautiful letters to Theo that summer and fall.

"The ones I sent in the summer were definitely more beautiful, whereas those done in the fall had it all over the summer ones in terms of their movingness, relatively speaking."

Vincent had the idea that Theo should become an artist too.

"'Who knows,' I said to him, 'you might even sell two paintings in your lifetime.' The look on his face made me instantly regret the remark. But it was too late to take it back, or say it again with any degree of spontaneity."

Vincent visited the newly completed Rijksmuseum in Amsterdam that October. He spent a whole day spellbound in front of Rembrandt's "The Jewish Bride."

"At 3:30 a.m., early in that whole day, I was alone, undressed, and on my knees before this masterpiece. Right there and then I performed a spontaneous circumcision on myself, a slow and painstaking process involving a total of two hundred and thirty seven paper cuts (the exact number of miners killed in France in the year 1875). When I ran out of pages torn from my untrousered copy of *Catcher in the Rye*, I started in on my collected letters. The expression on Bathsheba's sensitive and serious face never altered for a moment. It was as if she had discovered colour and divisionism in the same instant. The foreskin I have mailed to Mauve. Postage due."

In 1990 the sale of his "Portrait of Dr. Gachet" set an even higher record at $82.5 million.

"Oh boy, the sky's the limit."

Friday Reads His First Love Letter

dearest
most cherished friend

I'll come straight to the point, shall I
        we've come to the end

circumstances leave me no choice
but to return you to your pig gods
        if they're still interested

to your tribe
with its big drum
        its unspeakable
                                        appetites

(you talk in your sleep
did you know that
    —dear god!
how many nights)

go pour your eyes
spill the liquid of your hair
over another's breast
for all I care

I positively have no more words to spare

                    except

the day you learned to use a fork
(such concentration of silver
        caught up
in all that black)
you broke my heart

oh

and I want my umbrella back.

Siren at the Full-Service Station

In at last for that transmission leak, my focus drifts
to their calendar girl, stuck to a wall. Naked but

for plastic red pumps, flat on her back beside the sea on a
rock; knees asunder, inviting the sun. Avast, I'm gobstruck

peering through the porthole of a garage sailing off the
coast of Greece; flesh on a midday shore smothered in

a sauce of gold, snatching at men's interest on behalf of some
worldwide Maker of Tools. O traveller, remark this erubescent

beauty come to candle every small black day, light
fools the dusty way. Sealed eyes signify it's work

that satisfies. Hours wholly beneath her concern.
(It's my two mechanics who quote the standard rate.

And do I glean names from clots of cursive above their hearts
so's we can anatomize the weather together, me & Eddie &

Jim?) In time, the afternoon thins. My wallet sags
on its hinge (money gone soft, sluttish as skin).

Sent on my way, I get the complimentary nice day, and
the older, I swear, salts the air with a wink. But

think back on calendar girl, alone with her bones on that
blanket of stone. Those deathless open-toed shoes.

Excerpts from the Videotaped Confessions of Rumpelstiltskin

[concentrating on the long ash forming at the end of his cigarette]

You'll never guess it
so don't waste your fucking breath.

*[staring at the ceiling, both hands behind his head, fingers
presumably knit together]*

Okay, here's one: name me after some kind of primitive moth-eater,
a night feeder, eyes from the bottom of a well,
head inclined way back, pale throat a trap
set for the moon.

*[*a propos *of nothing]*

I've had women in high places
undress without me there,
licked whatever I wanted
from the windows of the fair.

[making and unmaking a circle formed by right thumb and index finger]

I think it's the way they come to me in parts,
pretending to be occupied elsewhere.

[looking directly into the camera]

Well my dear, just turn out your light,
cast into the night,
that long black rope
of hair.

[slowly rotating his head, as if from a stiff neck]

I know I tell it different each time.

But then, so do you.

[when shown photographs of the crime scene]

These are gold. Pure gold.

Cut from the body of the Monster's part in Mary Shelley's Frankenstein

When I reflect on all the hours wasted in front of the mirror, trying on faces....

To flesh out the details of my family tree I've engaged the services of a private investigator who moonlights as a sentimental novelist. The full implications of her status as the newest author of my existence have yet to dawn on her. The prose of her weekly lucubrations thus moves me more than words can express, especially a singular trust in such shopworn figures as "fervent longings" and "immortal lineaments."

I've started dance lessons. Mostly jazz. Some tap. Tuesday nights, from eight to eight-thirty. Well, to be precise, on Tuesday nights I spend a half hour crouched and peering in the window of a house in which dance classes are held. The people seem very nice, very light on their complicated ankles. But oh how often of late have I considered giving up these lessons. Frankly, I'm just not sure it's for me. I'll give it a few more weeks.

My heart doesn't beat on anything like a regular basis. Apparently, if you put an ear to my chest it sounds like cavefish arguing over money. A spelunker told me that, the only spelunker I've ever actually held in my arms. He didn't die well at all.

The cursed truth is this: though I'm actually a *42 Regular,* I wear a *48 Long* owing to a quite disabling self-consciousness regarding the vivid stitching of my extremeties. I have no wish to advertise myself abroad as the unsuccessful, albeit spectacularly determined, instrument of my own extinction.

Just at the moment I'm seeing someone who's really very sweet. She works with people with special needs. The silk of her throat, trimmed with soft blue shadow, strikes me as especially vulnerable.

With my rotten colouring I simply cannot risk pastels.

My left leg is subject to a peculiar twitch. Like a dog running in its sleep. My suspicion is that it secretly dreams of its former life. How else to explain the curious fact that I never appear in my dreams with my left leg. Once in a dream I went hopping through black fields after a dog escaping with what looked like a left human leg in its mouth. The dog then disappeared and I awoke to discover that my left leg had fallen asleep. In a rage, I snatched it in my powerful hands and set about shaking the traitorous dog from its unearned rest.

They call me the wanderer, yeah the wanderer, I roam around and round and round...

At this moment, my left hand hasn't a clue as to what my right hand is up to. Oh, why can't I be like other men?

From the very eve of my perfidious conception, the most private in the unruly parliament of members that is my corporeal frame displayed a temper too easily inflamed. Sometimes, I confess, I cannot resist teasing it myself, calling it "The Little Prometheus." This gets it going to unusual lengths.

When I consider all I might accomplish if people would only take the time to get to know the inner me. Yes, I have murdered the lovely and the helpless; I have strangled the innocent as they slept and grasped to death his throat who never injured me or any other living thing. But let's not forget: I was under considerable pressure.

I am a firm believer in reincarnation. I am. I am.

To aid in provisioning my unspeakable activities abroad, I vend original folk art from stalls set up at the sides of all-but-forsaken thoroughfares. My green bottle, with certain of the smaller bones of the human foot inside, each individually wrapped with a single thread of human hair and the odd fishhook, is probably my signature piece. The latest version I call "The Last Bottle You'll Ever Hold Up To The Light And Say What's All This About Then, Number 77." People still appreciate craftsmanship.

To this very day I remain convinced that, of the two of us, I wert by far the more eloquent.

Tomorrow I go to the bushes just beyond the schoolyard, where I'll attach a yellow eye to the children chasing each other over the asphalt, convinced the sun loves them, that the invisible seams securing their worlds shall hold.

To the hour of my exit from this ignominious stage of sorrow and despair, it shall remain my firm conviction that man is no more than the sum of his remarks, a temporary if surprisingly sticky concatenation of the found and already-fashioned. With some reservations.

If I'm ever trapped alone in a frozen waste, I pray I'm soon reduced to consuming my own parts. Thus by slow if inexorable degrees might I, in silence, dwindle to a self.

The World is Everything That is the Case

We have to assume that in a kingdom beyond the mountains a queen under a curse weeps tears of ice.

And that in what is widely seen as a cynical effort to finish the set, she has two similarly afflicted sisters (who do, as it happens, finish the set).

The lust of the Chamberlain is so impossible that highly-coloured birds ride the warm drafts upheaving from the palace's innermost rooms in an effort to draw him out.

Because these people have no definitive term for war, spontaneous gatherings outside the city gates are not uncommon. Among the uneducated this is called 'stirring the pot when you're still eating.'

The best dinner wines are fermented from the dead and are sweeter than guests have any right to expect. When the dead are unavailable their clothes make a bitter substitute.

Large numbers of children who've refused to become adults announce secret meetings in one another's homes, literally at the drop of a hat.

The source of the curse on the queen and her sisters is widely reported to be a remark made by a cooper after he mistook the hour and arrived home so late he happened upon himself leaving for work. Those who chanced upon the original event will claim to their dying day that it gave them a genuine moment's pause.

The Chamberlain has his eye on the queen and every last one of her sisters. Perhaps for him alone the sound of tears hitting the floor when they put their uncommon heads together is nothing like the sound of small pellets of frozen water striking green marble from a distance of just under two metres.

Apart from the fact that he suffers from fantastic mood swings, almost nothing is known about the King. This fact has all but guaranteed him pride of place among the most nominally interesting characters in the history of the universe.

Because every horse in the kingdom walks backwards even the longest journey demands a studied carelessness.

Finally, it is written that moments after reliable directions to this kingdom are finally committed to paper, it disappears with a trace.

So Rarely in Our Skins

I don't care if we're fugitives,
we are ceaselessly exalted, rising
like the drowned out of our shirts...

—Denis Johnson

World Series

A glance at that dark, unstitched wound and a deep fissure in my brain opens up; all the images and memories that had been laboriously or absent mindedly assorted, labelled, documented, filed, sealed, and stamped break forth pellmell....

—Henry Miller, *Tropic of Cancer*

oh
henry
that expatriate cunt
when he still boasted hair
shouldered into those great thighs
facing the funk and smack of tragedy
anticipating of all things the birth of stan
the man unusual laying down a bunt
out toward the mound
hellbent for first
arms and legs flying
the crowd a mess of folds and brainless
mouth crying like a child later in the dressing room
head in hands *those bastards think they own you*
time pinching his shoulders closed
leaning over the spectacle
of his rotting feet
his storied heart
a sinking
fast
ball

Werner Korsakov Says Hello

In my old man's country, the outlying
districts have shut down; roads overgrown, dwellings
derelict; soft grey sides in uncombed fields, folding
in on themselves. No one visits long or travels far
in that atmosphere, clouded and yellow most days.
Shadow turned to fluid in a jar.

For the last twenty years or so, he took his comfort
in the garage, mickeys of vodka stashed
wherever light was especially weak.

But you have to admire his longterm commitment
to the exercise, the way he had to form
his mouth before and after
each burning gulp of transparency.
I'll just be a minute, he'd say on his way out,
already half gone.

His liver eventually poisoned his brain,
leaving conversation to circle the present
like a bird whose legs have dissolved.

This is good, he says from the bed
in the permanent room,
new pair of slippers on his lap;
open-mouthed, blue velour, the short-term memory
of souvenirs.

But now everything is.

In poems death

In poems
death will find a way
                    to *breath*
or vice versa

oh maybe not easily
but always
in the end

as if the two were the oldest of friends
separated for the moment in a crowd
at one of those lively country fairs
(where, say, the cast from Josh Logan's *Picnic*
gets mixed up with figures
out of Brueghel)

each searching out the other's eyes
then working through the human crush
rubbing and laughing
their way together
because
            well

it's warm

light pulls at everyone's skin

and the balloons
can hardly contain themselves

This Morning on the Phone

                    my mother tells me
that her oldest sister, Margaret, hospitalized
from a fall at ninety-two
          and failing,
might lose a leg to gangrene

to save it they're bringing in maggots
from California

they eat only the diseased tissue
my mother, a nurse for thirty years,
is careful to explain

thereby starting my eye across her kitchen floor
down the stairs and along the shelves
behind the basement freezer

back into her old medical texts, catalogues
of vivid disfigurements into which I happened
a child holding on tight to a red crayon

they must be flying them in
is all I can think to say

too far to crawl she says
meeting me halfway

Fox Poem

it can start from an uncle dropping
somewhere in his prime
and a fox left behind
in an upside-down aquarium
formed alone along a shelf
        stopped once and for all
        in a box of air

as in life the head twists
slightly at your approach
as if hearing for the first time
        what works matter
        from skulls

one front leg hestitates
unwelcoming the ground
eyes nothing less than absolute

it isn't the bloodish currents of fur
      pried into life, not the black ridges
      of gum, death's sideshow grin

but you in the field those glass eyes fix
which unsettles

dust starting through buttonholes
    slow thinning from cuffs

mouth worked open

Two Photographs Taken by an Uncle Who Never Came Out

stepping from these small plots of lost ground
leaving the odd shadow of doubt

(on the camera's other side you'd only be caught
dead, minding that man's life)

here, then, your head draped like a secret
over the shoes of farmhands

(just boys, really, leaning in together
caught in a terrific blast of sun)

and here, finally, you thin as ash in the lap of a wife
empty hands folded in shade

hold it, you would have said each time
because it was how one played that game

as if any of us had a choice
when the actual moment came

Memento Mori

for Doug and Kathy

I

we have this set of tinted photographs of our parents
the two of them preserved under glass
taken together and apart in 1948
a few years after the war

studio pictures of their wedding day

they wore their cheeks glazed
as was the fashion then
pink rubbed into the bone
the teeth soft as if soaked
in too much light

the bride in ruched sateen, the colour green makes
when it's forced to stop

the groom a character actor
in a kiss-my-ass moustache

because these are tinted pictures
the embalmer's and the photographer's art
have come, as it were,
face to face, after the fact

the eyes are constant
because they are empty

there is nothing under the clothes
but a theory of form

and who could ever move from such air
(the consistency of wax or creamed stone)
let alone attempt to breathe it

not even after the nervous throat clearing
that little joke he would have planned
when this part was finally over

gifts left without a sound
unopened at their hotel

Axe Handle

Christ, you had it in you to be a holy terror. Anger so large
it stopped the air in the house for hours. Years.

Remember the only story you had to tell, to go with the only
photograph you have, of your old man? He's standing
in front of a barn, stuck in the marrow of an open door,
turning his white face from the camera,
smearing it against that day's sun.

In the story he's drunk as hell,
out looking for you in the apple orchard
with an axe. Kept you sitting up a tree freezing your ass off
that entire night. A boy no more than twelve alone
under the moon with all those naked hearts.

The time you told it, it was told as a joke.
And you couldn't remember,
not for the life of you,
what had set him off
that time.

And now you tell me that he killed a man on a train,
near Peterborough, with, of all things, a two-by-four.
An argument over politics. Long before you,
the last of eleven, was born. And then, by way of explanation, you add:
The Irish in Canada took their politics seriously,
especially then. Manslaughter. Did five years in the Kingston pen.

I thought you knew.

No. I didn't.

So let me offer something in return,
something I made for you. It's a picture of an axe,
handle thick as a two-by-four. I've left room
for raw knuckles. Several sets.

It represents that difficult breath he made for you
that night in the orchard when it got so cold,
breath which every so often
you asked us to hold.

Men of Few Words

he's taken to wandering
the tumble of years

hardly a sentence that doesn't misfire
                trail off

but ask who was with him
          way back when
and he can unwrap names
like they've been stored in cloth

and when John Wayne arrives, in *Rio Bravo*, and Dean
Martin, and Walter Brennan, and even that kid
Ricky Nelson

he decamps to the loud set, worn spot
in the wilderness

among quiet men
small, flat, familiar eyes

Picture This

Black often represents death, as does white.
—The Dictionary of Literary Symbols

In the bedroom
where my mother did most of her death
her parents looked on from either side
of the television, smiles taken
late in life, younger than she was then.

Right up to the end
she lived for the news
going over with her mum and dad
what would happen soon.

On the dresser opposite, there's my mother
at the age of three, in a party dress,
back on the farm, bag of candy sealed
by a pallid fist, eyes lost because
she's looking down

The better part of a century
standing in one small place
while the yard in front of her house
turned to iron, the sky filled with ash,
extremities of white.

On my desk is a relatively recent photograph
she sent of herself. She looks very good.
Her expression says,
Nothing will ever change here.

The television is on in the living room.
My children are running upstairs.

In this small part of the world
it's time for the news.

The Skin You Wore

The skin you wore through cortisone years
has thinned to almost nothing now,
a papery set of veils that barely holds
the muddled, berried flesh of legs and arms.

We never thought we'd see you down
to so few and such awful careful steps.
But you forget the harm in moving
as you used to through the world, until

flowers open on your clothes.
So when you go, I promise I will not say
"She died," but that I knew a woman
of skin so fine she stepped out of it

one day before we even realized.

We Cremated My Mother

But I wasn't there. I was miles away.
In a completely different province,
in fact.

My brother was and looked through the little window.
It might have been anyone in there, he said, which
was a comfort.

I have a nightmare, my mother said, that I'm alive
but taken for dead. They're burying me and
I'm not really dead. It was her famous recurring dream.
Stick a pin in me, kids. Make sure. We didn't exactly
bury her, we buried the ashes.
I was around for that.

A small hole full of muddy water. We lower the urn
into it. Poor drainage, my father says.
Someone blames the water table, and who could argue
with that? My mother had no love
of the water. I believe they make them watertight,
is my big contribution. Maybe we should have run
some tests.

The Bible lying open in the minister's hand
is limp as an empty bird, charred and wet.
She is not here, he says, looking up.

Christ I hope not, is really my only thought.

Long Distance

Yesterday my brother
who's moved back home
for a few months maybe
to keep dad company
          ease the transition
phones to tell me the old man has taken
to calling out her name in the middle of the night

Once, twice at most, but relatively casual
like she's down the hall
          just stepped out of sight

Then nothing. Silence
          the black water of some small hour
closing over the house

Jesus

So last night I have this dream
in which my mother phones and we chat
and then I say
Do you want to talk to dad
and then there's this pause and she says *I have to let you go*
I'm dead

She hangs up and I'm awake
my heart trying to sit up in my chest
and all I can think is I have to let them know
she called

Missing

> *Here then are three worlds—night, day,*
> *and the night within the night.*
> —John Cheever, *The Journals of John Cheever*

Gone a year this month and I haven't the heart to go looking
in any of the family albums—too many holes in the story.
Tongue to one side, she cut herself
from photographs, crafting dense little scenes
of a crime. Sent us all wondering after a body
that, having disappeared, would insist on such a crude outline.
The faces she left intact were made to last,
lie fast against a wall.

Suspended in the dark hold of my disposable
camera is one taken the same week she died. *Oh no,*
she cried, thin arms lifted, the clock on the shelf
taking its white face in both hands. *Stop it! Not now!*
I can't have it developed: it's the only one I have
in which she looks herself.

The Dead on Their Small Wheels

captive in the parlours
the dead wait on their small wheels
like lavish ornamentals
under heavy coats of skin

if they have trouble placing us
moving past in sluggish currents
of distress
(resembling each other more
with each and every pass)
they keep it to themselves

a composure so monumental
it makes the heart thick
to abide this close

after a day or so of this
they are almost empty
but still in place

(beside the grave a big mound of dirt
will have fallen asleep under a green carpet;
no one accuses it of anything)

the dead stop listening
the moment the last brakelight drains
into traffic beyond the gate

what happens next is as follows:
the dead begin a slow undress
through every last opening
of their Sunday best

swim naked under the grass

just imagine the momentary flashes
of parts drawn into the dark
each after the other
and in every possible direction

except one

Unfavourable Stars

The darkest place, according to the Chinese proverb,
is always underneath the lamp.

—Charles Simic

Seizing One Good Instant

we can hardly seize one good instant
of sunlight for ourselves and hold onto it
in our minds before it turns monster
—Al Purdy, "The Smell of Rotten Eggs"

the freckles on the face of the friend
drinking mooseheads with me under hot afternoon sun
precisely here on the open terrace of the brentwood inn
are much more tenuous than I remember
but this we may put down to her two years away
under the lesser lights of england

what hasn't changed one iota
is the languid order of their descent
down the pale currents of her neck
through the open collar of her dress
to muster above then thin and scatter from
the lift through shadow of glabrous breasts
unmarked for the moment by the spray of a sun
that knows shadow like moment must soon come undone

At the Beaverbrook Museum

I

I saw you
framed inside what's left
turning your face away
from the walls
arrivals echoing
all directions
I saw you
eyes balanced on a bluff
of bone tipping
backwards
I saw you
old and running out
of options
pockets empty bladders
made you look like you'd
once given birth
to gestures
I saw you
occupying that vinyl chair
like you'd discovered its meaning

II

After twenty minutes, you sat down.
Your goddam feet were killing you.

Don't be silly: This afternoon
was not entirely
a dead loss.

The look you then rendered in that series
was wonderfully accomplished.

You've got that ancient thing
down to a fine art.

This would be a good place to be buried, you say,
resting your eyes on the quiet stone floor.

A Disaster is an Unfavourable Star

On Lil's balcony I'm introduced to her friend,
the one with cancer. She wears around her head
its radically thin tentacular scarf the black ends of which
this evening have a mind of their own. It's
travelled to her brain, someone said, easy as scissors
falling. Only a matter of time. *So hungry I could eat*
everyone's *words*, was maybe the third thing she said.

Night traffics in stars cold before any of us
was conceived; when this city was under a mile of ice.
Billie Holiday is in the living room. And we used to stand
in fields near here and shoot our target arrows straight up,
at the sun, lose sight of the odd one. It was an invitation
to breathe; taught us the certain virtue, on occasion,
of not looking up. *Stars,* she says at one point,
are just another course of radiation.

I pry open my skull. So few working propositions, such doubtful
ground. All truth is finally local, rooms of skin. Less than
thirty-six hours later and already her face is failing.
I wouldn't like to guess her present age. *And I might make love*
to you, I remember thinking at one stage, *if it comes to that.*
Imagine if we didn't know death, how hopeless
we'd sound.

High School Reunion Buffet

The fill of years since that tiny green organza one
has altered some the lines which held your glory in
as I and others must have done

Increasing through several homes and house-
holds *Oh and don't forget the two dipshit husbands*
you add *If you really want to do the math*

                    and thousands of small days which
                    as they opened must have parted something
                    hard against you, like stays

For, no question, there's a lot more of you now

I figure (still working out the math) somewhere back
you just put away those two husbands
Ate them, I mean, just like that
And you know what? Okay.
They must have had it coming. Anyone
can hear as much in your voice, how
both dipshits would have left
a black tobacco taste:
All I did was open my mouth and
Bang! in they went, both the same way
Haven't seen hide nor hair since

                    The years it must take to digest and pass what's left
                    of husbands such as these; the bundle of their bones
                    moves slowly through you, balled tight enough to hold
                    the copper rivets of their jeans

Pressing one round fist
against your lips
you allow some gas
and hardly wince which
as I was going to say
is a really good look for you

One Time

jeZUZ boys   feature the arrangement on that   pop merrily chimes
in out of nowhere   casting a backseat of eyes
headlong at the most likely skinful
                    bent over slippery lawn
yellows shorts   presenting high   shuddering
through waves of sun   pale arm descending
to take the moment's pulse

pellmelling past   windows down the warm gravel road to copetown
for one of its brownwater swims   rambler's radio breaking in
delivering jayne mansfield dead in traffic   out of the wide blue

pop said flexing his hand we shall not see her like again
the very afternoon leeches somehow squeezed
into brian's red bathing suit   dense as punctuation against his white
belly   bursting with detail the heart leaked

promiscuous as omens

just that one time

Remembering My First

Galore: My name is Pussy Galore.
Bond: I must be dreaming.
—*Goldfinger* (1964)

Well, I'm ready. Maybe it's time we met.

How about under a streetlight?
You remember the one on the corner
about a block from my parents' house?
I'll enter the old neighbourhood from the west.

Remember to have about your person
that certain something
real men are apt to detect.

Of course what you choose to wear is your own business.
Avoid bright colours and strong patterns.
I've read where natural fibres and soft lines
suit you best.

If it's raining, it will limit itself to a drizzle,
enough to make the sidewalks sexy (you know,
black and wet), wrap our conversation in mild static
such as might be playing on a distant radio
tuned to The Music of Regret.

The first story you tell me of your past
should feature the following: irony, foreign locations,
false papers, abandonment. I expect you
to work your history into the conversation
the way you'd normally poison a drink.

If questioned, my mother will swear to the following:
Sometimes I don't know what to think.

I may attempt to kiss both your cheeks.
I perform this maneuver badly, but
bear with me: I've started work on a series
of unlikely attachments.

I don't smoke but you should feel free to indulge.
I like what it does to a mouth.

By the way, it's okay if your name is Roxanne
or Samantha. If, however, you're in the country
on a student visa working as an *au pair* girl
for a man who knows the lay of the land,
your name is Helga.

Magda will do in a pinch.

And if we do it, I'd prefer we do it
standing up, a falling together of overcoats.
So far as the precise angle of entry is concerned
my strong preference is that you remain entirely open
to suggestion.

Oh, and if this kid shows up,
fists screwed into his jeans,
sort of haunting the middle distance
just shy of the reach of the streetlight,
I'm afraid I'll have to run.

We're not allowed out on a schoolnight.

Stelco Song in Three Parts

I

martucci or gratucci maybe sonny gratucci
legend had it the only guy ever asked
for permanent nights in the universal slab mill

picture a bum-kneed latin alan hale junior from gilligan's
island saying fuck like he gets a nickle every time he showed
the fucking new fucks the best places to sleep or miracles
of energy conserved from leaning just the right way
on a broom anxious to talk if he could get you to listen and

you'd remember pulling free from him
that astonishing voice no matter where they eventually
put you after that was sonny's way to stay in touch

snatches of country opera showtunes you name it
short bright ribbons perfectly pitched through
sluggish shifts of furnaced air

through the din
clean descending rhyme

Liquor in the morning
Liquor in the evening
Eat her at suppertime

II

Want to see a picture of my wife?

It will be a joke

For ten seconds at least
you fail to make it out
then two fingers
holding livid folds apart

You are taking too long

Whasamatter? Never seen one before?

You are taking too long

III

he brings her to a barbeque after a softball game
and even close-up she barely makes a sound

occupied in a series of incomplete gestures
quite apart from things

oh but you want beautiful old world manners
you should have been there for sonny
introducing the little woman around

Some I Think Do There Embrace

in the end
she will remain among the ones you knew
passing through an afternoon
disquieting sort of pretty   self-involved
someone else's friend

she wanted to stop the car and read gravestones
yes she'd read them she assured us
all over the world
a regular camp-follower
when it comes to the dead

I offer the one I most recall:
what you are, I once was
what I am, you will be

it certainly gave me pause
made the ground uneasy
as if I might suddenly fall through the dark
into a stranger's bed

well it wasn't a woman she concluded
moving off   drawn by a fresh grave
it's just not something a woman
would bother to have said

but
the clarity with which I imagined us
laid out together
down to the tangled arrangements of hair
on the satin pillow
beneath our quiet heads

Ladies Night at the Three-Mile Tavern and Grill

at this late
and passing hour
the wake of the young fireman
with the crisp new forearms
stirs the smoke of women
expiring on their own

some dark-eyed as widows
on the ledge of ruin

here he comes
bending over them
through air difficult as memory
hard to swallow as a knife
opening the soft combustion of their mouths

to deliver what every organ of the media
gets such a kick out of calling
the kiss of life

To His Coy Birder

I

being a poet I feel I'm obliged
to confess this at the outset
before we further press
your fingers travelling however diffident
through air: I don't know from birds
couldn't tell you a wren from a lark
(I guess this means you can have me
even while the sun squeezes whole shadows
from our unmade bed)
a starling from a grackle
(your grackle might be your starling for all I know,
or care)

II

I met a robin recently
hopping the lawn
noted another in a tree
singing along
and here's what I thought
That sounds familiar—
why
that must be the robin's song

And then I suppose I cut the lawn

(I *know*!)
But I can go after it for you
if you like
I think I know where it is
untouched at the edge of things
in a thicket of unnamed sound

III

According to my dictionary
there's a category of lark
called the titlark

The *titlark*!

Come, it's early yet
we might still make something
of its song

The Poet Places a Personal Ad

All day my eyes leak
and long into the night
soaking the pillow, if you like
and I sleep unsound, until the room
is drowned; come round like a tourist
belly up on the briny, ironized water
of a red sea, feeling, oh,
strangely like me.

(Did you notice how I drew you
into the bedroom, even as I pointed out
the sucking wound that is my bitterness, even as I
set intimations of mortality adrift in the Holy Land? And
that's just for openers!)

Would you like me to do such things
to...thee?

I promise not to make trouble if you read big books,
travel widely, get away on those really long walks.

Right now I'm imagining us both undressed.
Is it natural that you're wearing more detail? Beside you,
I'm barely a smudge. What is the source
of your perverse power over me? And why
are the ends of my fingers stuck in your mouth?

Do you imagine a closet alive with zippers,
harness, latex rubber, nipple rings, masks? Yes, you do.
Well, I do too. Perhaps now we can speak of something else.

Let me be candid: My sensitivities are legendary in some parts.

Is this really the place you want me to stop?
Boy, I could tell you stories. My heart is bigger
than a post office box. I am waiting for you.

I don't get out a lot.

Translation of an Early Draft of a Poem by Bashó

        ...last night I dreamt that you took
a bath in a blue room and wanted me
to film it. Later, you invited me
into the bath and I left the camera
running. What happened next
will remain a mystery because I completely lost track
of the camera...

At this point the blue room stands for the decay of possibilities,
a room in a painting by a pre-Raphaelite
whose name definitely escapes me.
And a kind of affluence.

The camera stands for detachment.
For most men are nothing
without detachment.

You represent my representation of you
and of course the cruel limits
of representation itself.

The bath is filled to the brim with the usual farrago
of displacements and condensations.

The less said about the mystery that remains
the better.

Have I left anything out?

Till Human Voices Wake Us

I

to make silence
the thing; and make it
sing

consider specific winter limbs
nerves ravelling
warp of knots tied
(black as blood in starlight
say)
to certain angles in the day

inside
birds circulate frantic announcements
or merely laugh
out names

as we too arrange
voice, hair, fingers, frames

II

what did we promise
one another
you must remember

didn't we say something about
desire
which got us off to such a flying start

the way the drowned
dive for the black bottom
before they are ruined

and white arms drift apart

Inversions of Other Travels

Tomorrow
you will remember something
that never happened.

—Michael Redhill

From The Collected Veils of Salome

The position of the phallus is always veiled.... It appears
only in sudden manifestations, in a flash,
by means of its reflection on the level of the object.
—Jacques Lacan

Veil 3415.05
On those fundamental occasions of skin
swaddled in the advice of aunts
bones folded in aprons yellow
as flowers thinned from
the paths of saints
whatever it takes
wear it like the sun
putting a man's shoulders
in its mouth
advice she practised
a syllable for each and every step.

Veil 3415.08
The first time she kissed it
his head disappeared between the covers
of the July issue of *Seventeen*.

Veil 3415.21
She favoured skirts
only on days of execution and fasting
because then her otherwise unremarkable legs
tended to go on forever.

Veil 3416.05
Finally she asked in all innocence,
"If I'm the dancer *and* the dance,
am I also the *dancee*?"

Veil 3417.45
Definite turn-ons included photography, silk, figs, horseback riding,
and certain elements of the Jewish religion.

Veil 4456.74

Because her eyes cast such blameless light, she was able to mount
several solitary expeditions deep into her stepfather's house,
to its dimmest recesses, its innermost cells. *I name this place*
—this particular scheme of rooms—The Penetralia,
she sang as she skipped around the heart of things
wearing only her go-go boots. *I like the dance*
it demands from a tongue, the juice
of its Roman roots.

Veil 5417.56

"In the final analysis, what do these two fine breasts
really amount to," she thought,
"Apart from me?"

Veil 6619.77

She was a child trapped in a woman's body
which naturally left her plenty of room
to maneuver.

Veil 6724.12

In the night sky for several hours afterwards
Herod's erection was visible as far away as the future Khartoum.
This so-called "miracle" was later revealed to be a collapsed weather
balloon.

Room with a View

Late into every night, Penelope carefully undid almost that whole day's
work,
then slept with her fingers moving deep within herself to keep them supple;
that was the best and most dangerous secret of all.

The design of the tapestry never varied but each day she was a little different;
thus by degrees she flourished and the suitors had only their suspicions;
that was the secret every woman knew.

All those years, she stood for absent husbands, keeping other men at a
distance,
and the endless opportunities open to an intelligent woman left on her own
in a small apartment above reproach.

When Penelope looked at Telemachus, she saw only his father's faraway
eyes;
when Telemachus looked at Penelope he was sure he saw right through her.

The subject of the tapestry was tapestry. Only her women understood,
but even they thought it pornographic because it so excited them.

Odysseus filling the doorway, brilliant in the blood of every available rival,
took one look at it and said, *I see. I'll wait for you downstairs.*

Well, that's it, she said to herself, *I'm finished. And what would be the point,
after all, now that he's home?* But then she just sat there, staring at her work,
hands at a loss,
eyes swimming through seas of their own.

From Helen of Troy to Odysseus, Camp of the Greeks

hoping this finds you

my isn't rain a relief
after so much dust

they have a saying here
(by now you must have heard it)
                    a letter is a kind of prayer

but let me come to the point
              how much longer do you figure me, spear-prize
for these towers   these topless walls
neon-breasted   bride on all sides   hung up
between nights smeared red   and spiders
working a blue gap of days
in my head

from my bed
do you have any idea how diminished the argument
              how dismal arrangements
on the plain
        the River Scamander little more than a famished vein

                    oh yes I know   the gods gather there evenings
                    when they're done washing blood
                    from burnished legs   backs bending the soft metal
                    of the sun

                    (right   now pull the other one)

as you know friend beauty like mine travels well
but the beautiful (will you be one of those
for whom my silence was studied)
often end in such small worlds

(Troy, this imaginary city of the east, crawls with girls
drawn to its runways from the four corners
        city famous for its crushed feet)

beauty is a skin
stretched over the end
of every tactic
        don't you think
                (evenings here   after the hostilities
                the talk is to make a quiet killing
                in prophylactics)

remember your thousand painted ships
  bright as the hole made in a daughter's breast
        your terrible bird and thunder
instruments
all of you massed   missile-eyed
under splashing crests

and think   your occupation has become
                not to put too fine a point
        an occupation
(have you noticed of late
how indifferently the dead are undressed)

which brings me at last to my point

might one make a suggestion
regarding a way in (or out
depending)

you're the clever Greek   no stranger to deceit
so I put it to you

      think of one last empty promise
      victory curled in the belly of defeat

oh stop thinking woman for once

start thinking hardwood
and horseshit Greek

forever yours   I'm afraid

anxiously awaiting

I remain

Polyxena's First Love

> *Polyxena was the youngest daughter of Priam and Hecuba. During the time when the Greeks and Trojans gathered together in peace for the funeral rites of Hector, Achilles spotted Polyxena and immediately fell in love with her. After the fall of Troy, she was sacrificed by the son of Achilles at his father's tomb.*
>
> —*The Encyclopedia Mythica*

at the funeral my sister
pointed their hero out

really not the sort of shoulders I'd come to expect

I was looking for muscles
vegetables close-packed in skin
    not

silk emerging from soft watery-green breastplate
exactly like in that *Classics Illustrated* comic book
over which my brothers pored

normally their helmets hide their looks
eyes spark in the narrow gloom
beneath the crests

so I concentrated on my brother's empty armour
at the feet of this man
whose eyes went
everywhere

feeling his attention I must have put a hand
to my throat   the heat from the pyre
left a chill whenever it shifted

        anxious hot curtains of flesh

I remembered how he'd left my brother at the eastern gate
after their long evening out
dust deep-driven into
nakedness

after the city fell
his ghost came looking for me

at first I took it for smoke
but it followed and made me cold

yours is the black blood of a pure girl
it whispered against the thin walls
of my neck

            and you know
                    it's odd
            but I'd never thought of it in quite that way
            not once in all my life

then a boy was doing all he could to my heart
with the end of his father's knife

Clytemnestra on the Death of Cassandra

White shoulders parting like wings
beneath the axe. Narrow, it struck me,
as a child's, the cage of ribs breaking open.

But of course I was told she was on speaking terms
with birds; so that too was in my head.

He died like a warrior, in strenuous stages.
She collapsed all at once, like a bride; sprayed blood
like her body had starved the sun.

The smell of his insides in the warm water
was precisely the smell of birth
or food.

There was no attempt on her part or mine to turn from this.
There was nowhere else. We were joined in our resolve.
She knew exactly where to kneel.

The worst part was this: afterwards she seemed asleep
thumb folded up inside a fist.

What else could I offer a daughter whose throat would not close?
The father whose hand covered her mouth
to keep forgiveness in?

She was embraced as a member of the family,
welcomed to the small end
of something very long.

Men have called me a 'man-hearted cunt' for years.
In return I gave them all the gift of hindsight
and of prophecy.

At the Invitation of a Kept Woman

It is probable that originally Demeter and Persephone
were merged in one and the same individual.
—*Larousse Encyclopaedia of Mythology*

She's on the phone in the bedroom
alone at the high window, a fingernail absently
tapping the thick smoked glass, when Hades enters.
Before and beneath her on a sallow plain whole populations
are assembled for no particular purpose or end. As far as
the eye can see. If she turns away or allows her
concentration to lapse, she knows no surface
in this scene will either alter
or relax.

The air conditioning makes the sound of countless individuals
efficient at thinking the same thing.

She is wearing her grey sweater set and a smart new sable skirt.

Have you seen my briefcase? asks Hades. *I'm sure I—*

Placing a hand over the dark mouthpiece
her mouth forms a single word:
Mother!

The receiver is shaped like a jawbone of a hero.
She has been meaning to replace this model
with something a little less literal.

There isn't a moment of real colour anywhere on or near these grounds!
she cried the day she arrived.
Be honest, do you have any actual idea,
*just to name a colour that—oh, I don't know—*springs *to mind...*
I mean, are you aware of just how many possible shades
one has at one's disposal in the category
of green? Green alone, I mean.

They stood together before the anthracite house,
the small overnight bag against her side
soft and sad as a tumour.

And is this supposed to be the lawn? It's not a lawn, it's an ash-heap
flattened—or so it looks—by someone wearing spiked golf shoes.
The short dismissive sweep of one arm
pinned her words to the air
like empty gloves.

Why would you say 'someone,' replied Hades evenly
when I have legions at my call?

After a perfectly dead silence she said, somewhat under her breath
and smiling a little in spite of herself, *Technically speaking,*
the shades of green are likewise without number...
also, that is.

Thus was she fastened to the heart of the ruler of the Underworld,
like lichen to a naked rock.

I'll be home for Easter. Yes,
I promise. No, he's not coming. Don't start with me,
mother. Why do you constantly put me in a position
where I'm obliged to choose?

By the way, while I have you on the line, were you aware
that my name translates as either signifying 'dazzling brilliance'
or as 'she who destroys the light'?

I looked it up is how. Well, which was it
you had in mind?

Mother?

In Persephone's mind, her mother and their common past
would always smell of distant blooms
and the shadows they cast.

Mother, listen: why don't you come here? Seriously.
We have plenty of room.

Orestes in Oakville

Apparently the redoubtable Furies
from their earthy nidus disinterred
glommed onto me here, across a world
by way of a doomed credit application.

Figures.

Now here they sit
day after bloody day
knees tucked under chthonic chins
relentless on my couch
rending cellophane skins
from unwholesome snacks
one wide slick of unwelcome dank
that cut through the scotchgard
after the first few hundred
Hey why don't we just order ins?

O how they task me
task me down the length of these days.

How long, dear god, how long
since they fairly scampered to the window
            day or night
fingers spreading over the pane
after every ambulance howling the streets for gore?

Tonight I know they'll have me up all hours
each urging the other on
but only to gut familiar theme
            Clarity they'll moan
And a sense of purpose, however dire!
And the way mornings wrapped temples in light!
And how man's fear smells like salted bronze!
And how Bill Murray kills but has pretty weird skin for a star!

And they will lift those great heads a shade or two
at the perfectly regular way sirens can start in
            grow round
then narrow safely into nothing
away from them.

Bad teeth behind long fingers
one or another will suddenly ask
in a voice sufficient to dry the hinges
on the door
What are we doing here?
            Waiting for?

Ah...excuse me, I'll put in.

Then O they'll moan,

            It's him!

A Scorcher by the Pool

...the sun shone
As it had to on the white legs disappearing into the green
Water...
—W.H. Auden, "Musee des Beaux Arts"

these years arrangements at the deep end are coming along
swimmingly   won't you join me   (sorry
it's just that these days seem ripe
                                        for a plunge)

but doesn't one inevitably turn to the young (and here I generalize)
who dive right in   pry the sky apart   finish
               with such a neat splash

here one might recall the birth of dawn (such a mess of vein)
and work forward to the fact that any exodus from air
however monumental, involves severest strain

(but I digress) hours have always dressed in melting wax
fashioned gauds from the joints of kings (didn't sunburned Rameses
smite all the candles of the world with a single breath)

my eye was only following the children
the casual spill of their tracks

holes opening in their backs

their slow fall through sunlight
softer than ash

Naussica

The name of Icarus's girlfriend was Naussica,
so named because her father, an avid reader,
never travelled much and
from the first day of his married life never once looked
at his wife without thinking, *Good god, I need*
to get away.

Naussica was an acrobat, trained to vault
from the red backs of charging bulls. *But only one*
at a time, she'd always insist, the slender column of a finger
holding up the skies. *You should try jumping between my horns*,
Icarus would invariably add, extending his arms. Her eyes
always lifted at this, and never failed to execute
a memorable landing.

To stay in shape Icarus spent his afternoons running around
the tops of the walls of The Famous Labyrinth, incidentally
tormenting the Minotaur, famous for the dolls he made
from human remains. The Minotaur who
together with a poor memory was blessed
with an indifferent sense of direction
would often come upon his own creations
unexpectedly. After a roar of deeply-felt delight
he would bend to examine the work,
marvelling at the thoughtful knots and oddly moving
parts. *This is a found poem*, he'd think,
his thick tongue twisting in his head like
a rock dove caught between slices of bread.

Then one especially bright morning—so bright
that lizards passing too quickly over a shadow's edge
opened—the Minotaur and Naussica, each holding down
one lower corner of an immense imaginary isosceles triangle
suspended over the city, observed Icarus
undertake his fall.

Both struggled to find the right metaphor while they still had time.

Why, it's a bird, a bird dreaming it's earthbound...that it's a man, thought one. *Or a woman,* thought the other. And then, as is so often the case, their hearts kept right on beating, stirring together the several strong colours of feeling they felt into a not-unfamiliar mass of greenish-grey, because, much as happens to this very day, many things were abruptly coming to an end
just as others were finally getting underway.

The Torturer's Horse

Saturday last a young man passed
which sent the school sailing through to the next weekend,
flags at half mast.

According to this evening's paper, city council
has made up its mind: Hallowe'en is moving
from Sunday to Saturday night,
and that, my friends, is final.

An hour after closing, drunk and on the edge of a roof
several storeys high, urinating into the street.

Our chaplain works out of an office utterly bereft
of windows; by all reports, his door is always open.

"Took a header," is how one rosy-eared acquaintance of his
described it. "Pissed and pissing."

Head canted back, taking a long last drink of stars
is how you might imagine him, a gesture almost certain
to cost him his balance.

Long after the body of Icarus washed up on the beach
the fact that wax floats was widely regarded as vaguely ironic.

When they told him the terrible news, his father cried out
"My heart is wrecked." Doubtless words to that effect.

Icarus Lived on as The Incredible Falling Man

A headliner once, his posters read:
Headlong from so many storeys
in burning pajamas
to an ultramarine
sponge!!

Hits so hard he aspirates a limited series
of small grey clouds

It's an awfully fine line between flying and falling...
he'd whisper over the heads of the crowd
at some godforsaken fair
before lifting his arms in the air
taking the plunge
...the line that connects a wing
to a prayer

The Human Cannonball was asked to describe the sound: *Loud?*
Mother of god! Y'ever hear a fresh lung fired from a howitzer
intercepting a hot-waxed ford galaxie going ninety per
through a wall of marbled cheese?

Threw his leg over the Fat Lady
the winter she took up singing
heard the call
God gave us women the lay preacher explained
to help break the fall

Actually my father wasn't a geek his estranged son insisted
If I saw him at all
it was as a failed funambulist
Geeks bite the heads off small animals
like chickens
which are neither clean
nor especially bright

The act was billed
    the miracle of gravity
because his age had long since squared
the old circles of flight

Pneumonia his doctors concluded
We think it's time to send in the clowns

Cremation he answered when asked
I've never had much of a feel for the ground

Thus at last was he sent into the sun
    rising slow and alone
from a ramshackle   tumble-down
                    circus of bone

Pre-dawn Flight Instructions

Remember: between what we know
and can imagine is our true heading,

slurred ground, gravity unsound, where we melt
in dreams, in the dark, in silence, over water.

But if there's trouble, son, cast your mind
like a spear through the vanishing point.

Only a fool doesn't feel a fool
at the start of a long flight, he added

as he tightened my straps. *And looking down*
amounts to looking back.

* * *

A night bird shrieked above. Omen or prophecy?
Father assumed it named our wealth of apparatus.

I saw a small mouth open under one greater,
hooks shutting down a breast.

How Icarus Dreamed the Night He Departed

fretwork of aluminum

thin-skinned as the future of aviation

delicate as the first vapour trail

shiny hot muck from the wings

infinitesimal threnody

limbs suddenly wild for correlatives

long high thread of a whistle that reaches home
lifts a dog's head

flat bone of the moon
caught in a tree

small stone
thrown by a boy
gone back to sleep
in the sea

Notes on the Poems

The information on Kepler, the material in quotation marks, and the title of the poem, are from Evan S. Connell's essay, "Abracadastra," collected in *The Aztec Treasure House* (Washington, D.C.: Counterpoint, 2001).

The title "We do not explain pictures, we explain remarks about pictures" is a sentence from Michael Baxandal's *Patterns of Intention: On the Historical Explanation of Pictures* (New Haven & London: Yale University Press, 1985).

The title "The World is Everything That is the Case" is from Wittgenstein's *Tractatus Logico-Philosophicus*.